TANA HOBAN

I Read Signs

Harcourt

Orlando   Boston   Dallas   Chicago   San Diego

Visit *The Learning Site!*
www.harcourtschool.com

This one
is for
all my
children

*With many thanks
to all the sign-finders*

This edition is published by special arrangement with
HarperCollins*ChildrensBooks,* a division of HarperCollins Publishers, Inc.

Grateful acknowledgment is made to HarperCollins*ChildrensBooks,*
a division of HarperCollins Publishers, Inc.
for permission to reprint *I Read Signs* by Tana Hoban. Copyright © 1983 by Tana Hoban.

Printed in the United States of America

ISBN   0-15-326504-3

2 3 4 5 6 7 8 9 10   026   04   03   02   01